flash pan

poetry©

by Elliot M. Rubin

Copyright September 2018
Library of Congress

ISBN 978-0-9981796-4-3

Dedication
To my grandchildren
Shane, Isabelle, Jonathan, Carter,
Alexandra, Melanie, Mollie & Madison

In Memory of
Herman S. Rubin
Who wrote poetry all his life.

A Special Thank You
to Eli Langner
for helping edit this book

preface

When you see a magic show and are startled when there is a burst of energy in the form of smoke and a loud bang, it is due to a prop called a flash pan.

Thus the name of this collection is due to the urge to write a poem upon hearing a phrase or word which suddenly brings on a train of thought.

Imagination enables me, sometimes, to place myself in a situation mentally, and write about it, without actually having participated in a particular event.

Please sit back and enjoy my experiences, both real and imagined.

Table of Contents

you're gone

a wild animal is not a pet
to be confined in a cage,
once free to roam
it can't be tied up

you flew with the eagles
and ran with the foxes,
unrestrained, you soared
reaching new heights

you are the flame
and i am your moth,
my heart flew at you
it had no choice.

i know why you left me
i loved you too much
i didn't let you breathe
i stifled you too long

a powerful storm

one day last year,
the weather channel
reported a massive storm
building over the ocean
and heading to shore

next evening
i walked to the boardwalk
and looked out to sea

in the distance,
i saw black and gray storm clouds
swirling on the horizon,
in a frantic dance over the ocean
while electric fingers stabbed down
igniting the sky at dusk

there are no ships to be seen
they are safe and secure in port
while the storm rages heading right at me

an hour later standing on the beach
the wind buffets my face

a light drizzle is starting to fall,
water is running down my neck
soaking my shirt

high waves are racing to shore
raging with fury as they breach the beach
one after the other in a continuous assault

watching the surf crest and crash down on land
spattering onto the grains of sand

dissipating its strength,
reminds me of an elderly
prosperous and powerful person
who bulldozed their way through life
regardless of who was in the way;
and now is about to enter eternity,
equal to every other grain of sand

the next year on the very same day
i am sunning on the spot where i stood;
this time, it is sweat running down my neck, not rain;
and the storm, like the powerful, is forgotten

clouds

i remember looking up
at the beautiful blue sky
while i held your hand,
and seeing white clouds waltz by
as they brought a peaceful smile
to your face

they seemed to hear a soft rhythm
as they casually passed overhead,
in contrast to the harsh grind of life
below, many of us must endure

yes, we had a good thing going

then the rain came
in a torrent,
sudden and severe
as we struggled to stay dry

you succumbed to the
dark gray storm clouds,
leaving me alone
and missing you

i can't look at the sky anymore
the clouds depress me,
and rampaging rivers now overflow
with the raindrops that fall from my eyes

country summer nights

at dusk, the windows are wide open
and the sweet smell of the fresh cut grass
floats in on a gentle, undulating breeze,
teasing my body to go outside

i hear the chorus from the pond
led by the croaking frogs
and the chirping crickets
as they sing the higher notes
repetitively during the night

my senses are raging
as i lie in bed
staring at the ceiling

i try to go to sleep
but can't

my eyes are heavy
as they struggle to stay closed

it is taking forever to sleep,
and it feels similar
to watching grass grow

decisions

stacked row after row
they are calling me
to take them home.
this is an addiction to some,
which one to select
and wear with pride?

high heels, low heels,
many with stilettos,
red soles, black soles,
and all never walked on,
they carry their uppers
in a rainbow of colors

there are clogs, sandals
and leather boots too,
with deep markdowns
cutting prices to the bone,
all waiting for someone
to make their decision

the marketplace of dating
is no different than this,
so many to choose from
and some do fit well

while others flit around
from one to another,
ill-fitting choices seem to
always be returned,
never deciding
to move on
to the next aisle
over there

parents

outside it is pouring rain and
lightning flashes blind me,
since your passing years ago
there are thunderstorms
in my heart

aging

what was his name?

i knew him
for so many years,
his face is
right there
in front of me,
i can see it
clearly

i grew up with him

we played ball
on the streets of Brooklyn.

i remember his sister
and parents too,
and the home
where they lived

sometimes when i drive,
for a moment i don't
remember where i am going

slowly
slowly
slowly
my mind
is slipping away

antici...pation

my nerves are stampeding
as i try to control them
before they become apparent

this is my first time doing it

i previously only read about it,
and now reality is setting in

hopefully,
i will be ready

continuation

standing over the table
with a wet diaper in my hand
the baby below is struggling,
waiting for food

my daughter left
fresh breastmilk
for my grandchild,
who is screaming for a bottle

yet my aunts, uncles, and cousins
did not have living progeny
to continue their lineage

they lost their bout with life
in the woods of Eastern Europe,
when the spawn of hell
murdered them during World War II,
leaving the wolves, vermin, and vultures
to scavenge their bodies,
digesting and excreting
their chromosomes
on the death scarred forest floor

they did not enjoy life
liberty and justice for all

but a distant
small part of their
DNA still lives on
in my grandchild

in a land of immigrants

forever

since the beginning of time
it was grinding along
being crushed and shaped
below the earth's crust,
eventually, spat out and
exposed to the sun

it is now sitting
on the side of a country road
as a small elongated gray pebble
watching the world pass it by;
from its viewpoint
it seems very fast

yet its motion is none
until a young boy
walking by
picks it up,

skims it across a pond
watching it glide and hop along,
then sinking
among the fish and flora

its life in the sun has ended
never to be seen again

family

it was thankfully a sudden ending
because my mother died a painful death,
cancer ate the guts out of her lungs
while opioids gracefully closed her mind

being only sixteen i lost the love and
protection which held my world together;
mom's warmth enveloped me
as i grew up in her embrace

now i am an orphan with no siblings
aunts or uncles to take me in; only neighbors

mom said my father died in Viet Nam,
and she raised me as a single parent
in a small backwater town in Oregon,
surrounded by forests and mountains

going through her room afterward
i found a sealed box under her bed;
curious, i took out my pocket knife
and sliced some tape to open the lid

inside were old newspaper clippings
of an unsolved crime, a rape of a young
woman from Portland

the girl was not named,
but it pictured a bloody sweater
she had worn, and an emblem
sewn on the front was visible

looking under the loose clippings
i found the same emblem;

still attached to a piece
of bloody pink fabric

now i knew why my mother
had no other family around;
embarrassed and vulnerable
she fled as far as possible
getting lost in the mountains

resentful to be orphaned
so young in life
i forged her name
on one of her checks,
then sent away for a DNA test

there are few families
in my small town.
they took me in
until the state could come
and place me in foster care;
(if they were ever notified)

it took a few weeks until
the results came back;
holding the white envelope
in my hand
i carefully tore it open

finally, i discovered
if i would walk through life alone

or with family

fishing

he would get up at three in the morning
to drive to the bait shop to buy small
live fish to later put on a hook, then return
to grab a pole and hop into his boat

i was asked to go along many times and refused

as a young man, i preferred to go out at night
with my girlfriend, and then sleep in until noon

my fishing started at dusk and ended
before the sun set in the west

my lures of choice were the Red Devil
or Hula Poppa, both man-made and precluded
my getting up with the roosters

i remember casting my line
aiming for a lily pad in the River
Styx cove in Lake Hopatcong

as soon as it hit the water
a big bass jumped into
the air dancing on its tail fins

to be honest, it was unexpected
and shocked me from the solitude of quiet
in the cove with its suddenness

after that experience
i decided not to go fishing again

why bother the fish,
why bother at all?

keeping it real

i don't know why
i feel this way
every time
i see you

my heart
beats so fast
i can't contain
my feelings

you are so much younger,
my youth is flying back
in my ageless mind again,
yet my body is elderly

love
shouldn't
hurt
like this

should it?

drag racing on route 80 - 1963

the four of us left home one Saturday morning
a few minutes before the sun came up
the ride to the drag strip was on back country roads

along the way, we saw trailers carrying
dragsters, actually metal rails with a massive engine
bolted on a steel frame
also going to race that day

after filling up the gas tank with Sunoco
ninety-one octane the night before
my friends are going to race their
1958 Pontiac Bonneville

it was built with tri-power, but they took
off the three two-barrel carburetors
and put on a large Carter four-barrel

this car was fast

since i was not driving, i climbed up
on the stands to get an excellent seat
and watch the cars race down the strip

most of them were normal everyday
cars driven to and from work
or school; but the jet fuel dragsters
are deafening

loud is an understatement

with the drag racing bug in us all day
we all decided to race our own cars
on Interstate Route 80 the next day, Sunday

the road was being built at the time
and so far only went from the GW Bridge
to Netcong

we drove onto the eastbound lanes
and stopped,
with one car in each lane

then we raced

i remember her

we were only teenagers,
you were my sweetheart
to be mine forever and a day

with long brown hair
and a winning smile
how could I not love you?

i never could imagine not

you made the USA Teen finals,
a vibrant young girl
with star potential,
i was smitten,

but that was decades ago

i looked you up online one day
and was disappointed in what i found.
you didn't mention children
or family, or friends
only an expensive luxury car

you showed no empathy
for people
or feelings of kindness to others,
only bragging

i am wiping my memory
clean of you,
clearly
i am disappointed

it is time for you to go

i wanted her

throughout my public school years
i looked at her in mom's dining room
while struggling with my studies

she never said a word to me
only returning my glances
as i picked up my head
from my books,
for a brief moment of respite

i dreaded doing homework
yet was smitten with her beauty

perfect features finely rendered
with skin so clear
making my mind wander
as to her true identity

was she a courtesan in a royal court
or a wealthy beauty kept by her lover
copied for immortality in ceramic?

my mother collected antiques
and after she died, I told my sister
take whatever you want,
except her

as i approach old age,
i find myself still staring at her

entranced

lifecycle

in the springtime
flowers pop out of the earth,
slowly at first
then in bursts of color,
they bloom
for all to see and enjoy

their beauty is their work,
their colors our joy,
and small bees stealing pollen
help them to grow a new plant

our work is reproducing,
the continuation of species,
tilling the young
till they can bloom on their own

then we wilt with age
falling back
into the earth
to continue the cycle

love

when the deepest blues hit hard
and all i can see or feel is despair

i remember our embrace
and your passion sprinting through me

the warmth of your being cheers me,
i can see a bright future ahead for us

you give me something to live for
knowing true love never fails

marriage

dating is similar to a rubber ball,
it can go fast,
              sometimes
bouncing
          around

and may take time

to slow down a bit;

until it finds

the perfect

resting
spot

truism

although it can be fleeting
when it hits, it is intense

feelings of affection
are like a truck
hitting a wall
smashing into everything
sometimes destroying
common sense

there is a truism
no one can deny

when it is present
love conquers all

missed opportunity?

i did not like the way
she spoke to us

as a college student
i knew to keep quiet
and bite my tongue

i was here for an education

the next year she was fired
for sexual harassment
of her students

now I feel bad
that i was not
attracted to her

Mollie in Atlantic City

sitting on her father's shoulder
the carefree smile of youth
cannot be missed, with
a red bow pinned atop her head

the wind is
blowing strands of
loose brown hair
about her face
framing a smile
as wide as the sea

the boardwalk at night
beckons children
with the salt air
stirring them awake
and the crowds of people
walking by
in colorful clothes
catch her attention
driving away any
thoughts of sleep

finally
she bends forward
resting her upper body
on dad's head
as mom decides
it is time to go

but not until dad
buys an ice cream cone
to eat undisturbed

moving on

it is hard
to forgive you
the hurt
runs deep

maybe in time
we can be together
again

but not now

i don't know why
you did it,
you know how much
i love you

what i need to do
is wipe clean
my feelings for you

i need an eraser

number one

between the first and the last
there is a middle
with many life experiences
stuffed inside of it

there is a place in my heart
for you,
always there
in the background
comparing others
against my first

my mind dashes back
to the happy times we had
as i race through life,
because
you were my
starter wife

monster in the dark

late at night
i hear it roaming
around my ears
unseen in the darkness,
almost invisible
in the light

i know it is here

it's destiny in life
is to harass,
and tonight
it chose me

why?

what did i do
to this tiny monster
who wants my blood?

i gave at the Red Cross
support worthy charities
but no, it is not enough to warrant
a pass for a restful sleep

instead

i flip on the room lights
grab a rolled up magazine
then start the hunt,
jumping on and off the bed
trying to clear the sleep from my eyes

it taunts me

flashing by my ears unobserved
then disappearing somewhere
in the room

waiting in ambush

the next morning I see it,
bloated
with my blood,
tired and resting
on the lip of the sink

awaiting its fate

looking forward

i thought i would never say this

you have been with me
for so long
i can't remember
not having you always
at my side

yet nothing is forever

although i would like
to think otherwise
i need to deal
with reality

it is time for you to go

i loved my Brown Sugar,
for too many years
we were a couple

but my body
can't take you anymore,
at last, i am free
from your addiction

i threw away my needles

at a writers conference

i was mesmerized in class
while looking over her shoulder
from behind

at the notes she is taking
while the lecturer speaks

in a small notebook
her words are hand printed,
finely lined up and down the page
perfectly level and evenly spaced

as if a mechanical printer did them

she is a faceless blond
in an aubergine blouse
with wavy long hair twirling about
when she turns her head to look up

how unique i find her writing

intimidated, i don't tell her
how much i am astounded
at what she is doing

there is no way in this life
i could ever do that

at best my printing
is similar to a kindergarten
child doing finger painting

i remain mesmerized

my problems are overbearing

the storm clouds
are coming at me
i can feel them in my bones

the darkness is pervasive
as i sink further
into myself.

in a last gasp effort
for help
i reached out to you

and you responded
with empathy
and love

thank you

i can feel
the sun
on my face
once again

reality

gripping his bible in his left hand and
holding it tightly against his chest
he raised his right arm
high above his head
and shouted out to God

the mass of people
in the rural tent's stands
heard him preach his truth;
it is a mortal sin for people to marry
who are of the same sex

in unison, the packed crowd sang out... *amen*

at the same time a hundred miles away
in a small city hidden in a green treed valley
his daughter is saying her marriage vows

having dated a verbally abusive boyfriend
she met the love of her life at a parade
when their eyes first met across the crowd,
it was love at first sight for them both

tonight, while her father preaches hate,
she marries her wife for better or worse,
his daughter understands this truth...
there is no such thing as bad love

summer romance

i've kissed you a hundred times
always with passion and love,
holding you gently in my arms
in an embrace which never ends

it was a summer romance
so many years ago,
teenagers with unchecked
emotions running wild

decades have passed,
i see you all the time;
then the morning arrives
and my dream ends

with you leaving me
once again

the bed

lying in bed one morning
with a fractured leg,
too tired to grab my crutches
then, a slow walk, to the wheelchair,
my mind starts to wander

i can hear the birds
sitting on a tree limb
outside my window,
chirping a song
i can't sing along with,
yet it is melodious
when a few of them join in

when they fly away
the silence is deafening

my mind starts to wander
stirring up deep thoughts,
things i could be doing
instead of staying in bed

the question is
will i do them
once i am out and about?

or will i tuck them
back away in my mind
until the next time
i am stuck in bed?

wild west

in the old wild west of America,
many farmers tilled the soil,
and cattle roamed freely
on the vast open plains

horses were the main means
of transportation back then,
they were needed to round up
the herds, and to bring goods
and services to small towns
and big cities alike

buying and selling a horse is called
horse trading. it is pure bargaining,
never knowing if you received a
good deal or not

in today's world horse trading
still exists every time you go
into a car dealership

you never know
if you made a good deal
or not

until a friend
tells you
what they paid

empathy

as a teenager, she saw a flyer
for a beauty contest, and entered
hoping to win a chance to go
to the finals in California

after work, her mother would
sew fabric making her a dress
to wear for the big day

tearfully remembering
the anticipation of going
on the stage, she still shudders
after all these years have passed

sunning on a chaise lounge
by her in-ground pool, she is
slowly sipping her Pina Colada
with the cherry on the bottom

the Mercedes dealer will be
bringing her car back later after
servicing it, and the two housekeepers
are inside cleaning and cooking

things have changed,
sometimes
dreams do come true;
especially when the winner
of the contest gloated
you are not beautiful
enough to win

and is now inside cooking dinner

witness

when i look at open fields
with overgrown green grass,
scattered about
are small
purple wildflowers
swaying with the wind;
i wonder why?

looking overhead there are
birds swooping down
effortlessly riding air currents
that i cannot see;
something is enabling them
i wonder what?

in a small bedroom
a mother cradles an infant,
the combined parts
of the baby is overwhelming
as they work together
to create a person,
i wonder how?

some people say it is nature,
some say it is the work of a god,
of which there are so many

i believe it is the work
of a source of power
we do not understand

to that source,
i am a witness

word$ of wisdom

my bookcase is filled with all sorts of books,
with subjects from whimsy to poetry
to history, and even heretical books next
to my editions of Talmud and Torah

the question is why?

many years ago i mentioned to my father
there was a book i wanted to buy
but it was a lot of money

his response to me, i now realize,
was a reflection of his intellect

don't ever stop learning,
buy the book, take a class,
it's only money.
there is no
cost too great when
it comes to knowledge

writing

unlike death

writing never stops

until it is published

…or re-edited

memories are hard to kill

they spring up when i
least expect them,
surprising me, and sometimes
they bring a smile to my face

it has been decades
since we were together;
kissing, holding tight,
and never thinking
of letting go

the other day I dreamt of you
as i was in a deep sleep

(while unconscious)
it was so real
i could feel
your breath
on my face

and i missed you
all over again

zero

driving along a country road,
                       a squirrel ran out
as my car's tires reached
                         the same point
in the street
                        as the rodent

young children are attacked
by cancer,
innocent babies,
not yet out in the world
into which they are born,
suffer

sometimes
things just happen
you alone
cannot control

let alone change them

the truth is
there is nothing
you can do about it

and this fact sucks

personal values

they were a young couple,
he was handsome beyond doubt
and she was stunning,
either of them could be
called eye candy

well dressed and well spoken,
yet something was missing

after a long courtship
the couple broke up
then went their separate ways,
never to be together again

he moved far away to forget
and she stayed in town,
looking to start her life over,
without him

the problem was he placed a
value on everything, equating it
to money or time, with no regard
to her feelings or interests

one day she met another young man,
not as handsome or wealthy, nor
especially good-looking, but
kindhearted and caring about others

giving up a luxurious future
with flashy cars and homes,
she decided one day to be real;
there is no price tag on love

summer rain

massive storm clouds are rolling overhead

lightning and thunder shaking the house,

torrential rain is pounding the windows,

yet i feel safe and secure in your arms

coming home again

it is way past midnight,
you are lying next to me
with your piercing eyes open,
awake and thinking
about today's events

your silence is deafening,
i can hear you breathing

what happened was beyond
our control.
we knew their
marriage was doomed
before it even started

soon our child will be
back home, ready to start
over with someone else,
adding to the tensions
in our life,
carving
new worry lines
on our face

the frost

summer is in the past,
with our running around
and playing together
in the water, memories
of a time well spent

soon winter will be here
with the foraging critters
hibernating in the woods;
while we sit comfortably
in a heated home

as we look out at the
white crystals of ice
bending the green grass shafts
downward
with a gentle touch,
almost reaching the
cold frozen ground

the late fall frost
changed
the cheerful
summer colors
to brown,
awaiting a quilt
of white
yet to come

vote

it does not matter
which city street is shown
on television
there is no color,
only tinged grey
from the buildings shadows
washing everything with sadness

it does not matter
the color of the child,
boy or girl, infant or teen,
struck down for no reason at all
killed before they could live life

it does not matter
logic has no place on the streets
or in governing bodies,
money has precedence
over our lives

it does not matter
if i watch the news or not,
a parent's agony and tears
will not change anything

it does not matter anymore
unless we do something,
anything, to change course
and make ourselves matter

explaining

how do you explain
creativity to someone
with a plebian mind?

how do you explain
mental inspiration
to someone who
follows and
cannot inspire?

how do you explain
being different because
you have no choice?

how do you explain
there is no way to
explain these things?

enchantment at the bank

as i walk in the bank
this white haired lady
stood motionless
on the other side
of the glass door
waiting

thin
blond
blue eyes
blue hair, coiffed
nice clothes
flirty eyes
flirty lips
flirty face

i open the door,
she smiles
at me asking
if i opened it
because of her
age or beauty?

i answer her,
both

it doesn't matter
if she is flirting
or not

it is years
too late
for me
to care

the sound of the shofar

the shofar rings out, rushing in sweet memories
to my consciousness; i remember as a child
going with my father to shul and sitting on his lap
next to my Zayde, packed in shoulder to shoulder

looking to my right, i see a black cloth hung over
a white lattice wall, shielding my grandmother who is
sitting with other women praying. walking around to
see her I am greeted with warm hugs and kisses

hearing the blast of the ram's horn brings back
times and people long gone, with tears of sadness
slowly trailing down my cheeks, the warmth of
the love they gave me still resonates decades later

listen to the shofar
listen to your heart
listen to their voices:
they are still here

pests in the attic

when i sit down to eat
i hear them scamper
around in my attic,
directly over the kitchen table

i know what they want

to come down
and eat my food,
the New York cheesecake
i bought the other day,
creamy and smooth
with just a hint of lemon
on a graham cracker crust

the pitter patter drives me crazy,
i'm going to get them all
one way or the other

i call an exterminator
who refuses to exterminate!

he wants to set a trap, and
then close the outside air shaft
with a heavy wire screen
so they can't get back in

he said he is okay with killing ants,
so i told him about a few uncles i have

some people have
no sense of humor

reality at the horse track

i see him pull cash
from his right pant pocket,
in his left hand
is a racing form
with circles drawn around
the names of horses

the odds on the board
are moving fast
while he watches
them fluctuate

ash from a cigar
falls on his shirt,
sweat stained
from too many nervous bets,
losing ones,
one too many

this time is different,
he feels it
in his bones

after a few races
the floor is covered
with betting slips
feeling like a carpet
under his feet,
hopes and dreams
being trampled on,
then the losers
begin betting
on their next big win

on the track
the stalls are filled
with four-legged athletes
ready to run.

with the sound of a gun,
the gates open
and they scramble out

his bet is running lightning fast

around the last bend
he's in the lead
heading for the finish
and a win

people are jumping
up and down
yelling with glee
as the horse
comes in first

running to turn in
a winning ticket
he collects the cash,
then turns around
and hands it over
to a facially scared
large man
wearing a sports jacket
two sizes too small

he is paying off
old bets,
averting broken bones

senior Thursdays

she stops in the middle
of the aisle
blocking my path

i notice her
red, blue and pink
floral dress,
stylish thirty years ago

she looks at the red apples
stacked one on top of the other
in a pyramid

they are all the same color
with stems pointing up,
maybe a worm or two
drilling through a few,
when she turns
looking through the pile

people are lined up behind me
with their empty carts
eager to be filled,
yet she is oblivious
to the real world,
living in her own small reality

someday that could be me,
with drool slowly
slithering down my chin onto my shirt,
and a nurse
pushing me in a wheelchair
because it is Thursday,
trip day to the market

exercise

looking out my window
i see the golfers,
retired men and women,
walking with a club
in their hand
looking for a ball
they sliced to the right,
and can't seem to find

they think golfing
is exercise
when they hop on
the golf cart
and drive to the next spot
where they feel
their ball landed

i see them standing
on the grass pulling out
two wedgies;
one, a golf club; the other,
their pants from sitting
on the golf cart too long

the truth is they get more
exercise going from their car
to the clubhouse restaurant
for lunch,
then walking back to the car
and watching television at home
till dinner

civility

this was a business meeting,
and i made a mistake;
criticism is okay

but the yelling of gutter
language is out of line

i thought he was
a smart person
until i found out
he voted for
a thief and liar
for president

i left the meeting
when he cursed at me,
using profanity
best reserved
for a bar
or locker room

someone
ran after me
and said
he told him
he was wrong,
and should apologize
but he never did

did I know he had
cancer? he said to me

does this make it right
i asked?

i was informed
he needed someone
with a rare blood type
to save his life
in his battle against
a deadly disease

i smiled,
walked away
and said to myself

Karma is a bitch

sick kid

sitting in my car
during a thunderstorm
while my wife is in the
nail salon
the thumping
of the drops
on my windshield
reminds me of
when i was a kid
and had the measles

looking out the bedroom
window i saw the doctor
park his tan Lincoln,
with the suicide doors
in the middle,
open the driver's door
carrying his black bag
and head for my house
with needles
intended for me.

Measles…
he told my mother to
keep me out of school
and put cold rags on him

Stalinist torturer

house calls and measles
are like yesterday,
both are in the past
and hard to find today,
if ever

Other books by Elliot M. Rubin

A trilogy of 5 STAR crime/action novels
Hot Cash/Cold Bodies
Kara Bennet - Vengeance
Dead Girls Don't Die

Romance and Murder in Bensonhurst

Flash Fiction
People Stories in 600 Words
(as told by a raconteur)

Poetry
Scrambled Poems from My Heart
A Boutique Bouquet of Poems and Stories
Rumblings of an Old Man
Surf Avenue Girl and other poems

Jewish Satire
The Phartick Chronicles

www.CreativeFiction.net